MW00996993

Praise for
the ParentSmart/KidHappy™ Series:

"It is rare to find a book that teaches essential life skills to parents and children at the same time. These books are brilliant for parents who want to re-parent themselves."
—**Kathryn Kvols,** president of the International Network for Children and Families and author of *Redirecting Children's Behavior*

"These books present important concepts to parents and children. They can help children learn to be aware of feelings and to engage in problem solving, key components of emotional intelligence. The explanation of these concepts at the end of the book is also important for parents to be able to generalize these skills to other areas of the child's life."
—**Steven Tobias, Psy.D.**, coauthor of *Emotionally Intelligent Parenting*

"While the stories focus on encouraging cooperation in young children, they clearly serve to build confidence in caregivers who will appreciate the boost."
—**Donna Erickson,** host of award-winning *Donna's Day* on public television, author of *Donna Erickson's Fabulous Funstuff for Families,* and syndicated newspaper columnist

"ParentSmart/KidHappy is for any family looking for ways to get through those all-too-common everyday struggles. Reading these realistic stories together, kids and parents learn positive, hassle-free solutions to those universal battles."
—**Nancy Samalin, M.S.**, lecturer and best-selling author of *Loving Without Spoiling: And 100 Other Timeless Tips for Raising Terrific Kids*

"Wonderful . . . for both parent and child."
—**Michael Popkin,** author of *Taming the Spirited Child*

Ready to Play!

A Tale of Toys and Friends, and Barely Any Bickering

by Stacey R. Kaye

illustrated by Elizabeth O. Dulemba

edited by Eric Braun

free spirit
PUBLISHING®

To my mom and dad.
—S.K.

Always, for Stan.
—E.D.

Acknowledgments

Thank you to Michele Fallon, LICSW, for her valuable feedback on drafts of the book.

Text copyright © 2009 by Stacey R. Kaye, MMR
Illustrations copyright © 2009 by Elizabeth O. Dulemba

All rights reserved under International and Pan-American Copyright Conventions. Unless otherwise noted, no part of this book may be reproduced, stored in a retrieval system, or transmitted in any form or by any means, electronic, mechanical, photocopying, recording or otherwise, without express written permission of the publisher, except for brief quotations or critical reviews.

Free Spirit, Free Spirit Publishing, and associated logos are trademarks and/or registered trademarks of Free Spirit Publishing Inc. A complete listing of trademarks is available at www.freespirit.com.

Library of Congress Cataloging-in-Publication Data
Kaye, Stacey R.
   Ready to play! : a tale of toys and friends, and barely any bickering / by Stacey R. Kaye ; illustrated by Elizabeth O. Dulemba ; edited by Eric Braun.
      p. cm.—(ParentSmart/KidHappy series)
   ISBN 978-1-57542-318-0
   1. Play—Juvenile literature. 2. Friendship—Juvenile literature. 3. Child rearing. I. Dulemba, Elizabeth O. II. Dulemba, Elizabeth O., ill. III. Braun, Eric, 1971– IV. Title.
   HQ782.K34 2009
   649'.64—dc22
                                                                                2008031364

Cover and interior design by Michelle Lee

10 9 8 7 6 5 4 3 2 1
Printed in China
P17201208

Free Spirit Publishing Inc.
217 Fifth Avenue North, Suite 200
Minneapolis, MN 55401-1299
(612) 338-2068
help4kids@freespirit.com
www.freespirit.com

Grown-ups:

The language of positive parenting
in this book is color-coded.

Purple words invite solutions and outcomes.
Green words validate feelings.
Red words encourage.

Learn more about these techniques
at the end of the book.

The doorbell rings—Emma's
friend has come to play.
"Hi, Ryan!" Emma says.
"I'm glad you're here."

"What a nice way to welcome your friend," says her mom. "Look how happy Ryan is to see you."

Emma has been waiting all day to play castle.
"I'll be the princess and you be the prince."

But Ryan has a different idea.
"No, let's play store!"

Emma stomps her foot.
"I don't want to play store.
It's *my* house, and I say we
play castle!"

Mom helps Emma solve her problem.

"It's frustrating when you and your friend disagree, isn't it?" she asks. "What can you do if you and Ryan want to play different things?"

Emma grumbles, "Nothing. Play our own games, I guess."

"Yes, that's one idea. How might Ryan feel if you play different games?"

"He might feel sad we're not playing together."

"That's a good point," Mom says.
"What else could you do?"

"Um, we could take turns."

Mom smiles. "Go ahead and try that idea."

"Ryan," Emma says, "let's play store first . . . and then can we play castle?"

"Yeah!" Ryan cheers, and the two friends work together to set up their store.

Mom checks in on the storekeepers later. "Wow! Look what's for sale. May I go shopping?"

The kids giggle and give Mom some play money to spend.

It isn't long before Emma's tummy growls.
"Mommy, can we please have a snack?"

"When you say please, it's easy to say yes."

After a snack, Ryan and Emma go outside to play castle. Ryan picks up a toy horse, but Emma quickly grabs it back.
"Hey!" she shouts. "You can't play with Oliver!
He's mine!"

Mom tries to comfort them.
"Emma, I know how much you love Oliver. It's hard to share your special toy, isn't it?"

Emma nods. It *is* hard.

"Ryan, how do you feel when Emma yells and grabs the horse from you?" Mom asks.

"Mad!" Ryan yells.

"I'm sure you do feel mad." Ryan and Emma start to settle down. Emma's mom understands how they feel.

"Emma, can you think of something different to do when a friend picks up your special toy?"

Emma thinks for a minute. "I know! I can give Ryan a different horse to play with."

"Sure," says Mom. "Give that a try."

"Ryan, Oliver is special to me. Could you please play with Francis instead?"

"Okay," Ryan says. "I didn't know Oliver was your special horse."

The kids are having
a great time when Ryan's dad arrives.

He says, "Hey, big guy! Did you have fun with Emma?"

"I don't want to go home!" wails Ryan.

"I know how you feel," Dad says. "It's hard
to stop playing when you're having fun."

Emma has a great idea. "Ryan, do you want to take Francis home with you until next time?"

"Wow, thanks!"
Ryan says.
"Giddy-up, Francis!"

Helping Kids Get Along
And Raising Emotionally Intelligent Children

Learning to make friends and get along is a major task of early childhood. One of the most important ways kids learn is by playing with peers, which can be great fun but can also be challenging. Playtime conflicts such as disagreements, power struggles, and jealousy tend to peak by age 3 but can be a factor for years after that. How can grown-ups increase the odds for successful playtime with friends?

First, plan ahead. Brainstorm playtime activities with your child and make sure she understands that she and her friend need to agree on what to play. To avoid tension, you may want to put away any toys your child might have difficulty sharing.

During playtime, resist the urge to quickly solve problems for kids. Instead, let them try to work out conflicts on their own. If things escalate, guide them to a solution by asking questions rather than by providing answers. Encourage them to think about each other's feelings. Research shows that kids who learn to consider the feelings of others and figure out their own solutions to problems are more likely to grow in self-esteem, independence, and emotional intelligence.

The term "emotional intelligence" refers to our ability to recognize emotions in ourselves and others and to manage our emotions. Experts such as Daniel Goleman, who has written several books on the subject, consider emotional intelligence a key to developing strong relationships, an optimistic outlook, self-confidence, and general happiness.

When kids take ownership of their problems, they develop their emotional intelligence while learning to cooperate with friends and grown-ups. While no book can tell you exactly what to say to the children in your life, the following are basic guidelines recommended by psychologists and parenting experts.

Invite Solutions and Outcomes

When we regularly rescue our children from their conflicts, we unintentionally convey that they are not capable of solving problems for themselves. Instead of telling children what to do, ask questions that invite them to brainstorm solutions and consider outcomes. For example:

- What can you do when someone pushes you?
- What will happen if you grab the toy back?
- How will your friend feel if you don't let him play?
- What else could you do?

It's important to ask your child to consider how others might be feeling now, during the conflict, as well as how they are likely to feel later, as a result of your child's suggested solution. This helps children develop empathy and perspective—invaluable social skills that will serve them well throughout their lifetimes. It also helps them come up with the best solution: one that takes everyone's feelings into consideration.

When asking questions of your child, be careful not to criticize his responses or be too quick to provide your own solutions. Give him the time he needs to come up with solutions and imagine and evaluate outcomes.

Most kids get angry or frustrated when faced with their own challenges. Therefore it may be best to introduce this technique while reading books. Ask your child how characters in a story might feel when confronted with a problem and what your child might suggest to solve the problem. Then ask how the characters might feel if they follow your child's suggestion.

When your child is ready to solve his own problems, start with simple ones that do not involve others. For example, when he spills juice on himself, he can get a towel and change his shirt. When he drops a snack on the floor, he can pick it up, throw it away, and ask for a new snack.

In the main part of this book, look for dialogue in purple for examples of inviting solutions and outcomes.

Validate Feelings

Children who know that feelings are normal and feelings have names have an easier time managing and expressing them appropriately. Children who learn to recognize and manage their own feelings also learn to have empathy for other people's feelings. In turn, these skills help kids improve social skills and do better in school.

It's important to acknowledge the child's feelings even if you can't accommodate them. Letting kids know you understand how they feel shows that you think they and their feelings are important. A child who feels important is more likely to cooperate (with grown-ups and with other kids), have high self-esteem, and develop positive emotional health.

To help kids learn about emotions, talk with them about their feelings, your feelings, and the feelings of others. Recognize feelings, name them, and make it clear that all feelings are acceptable. It's fine, for example, to be frustrated if another child takes your special toy. It's natural. However, not all ways of showing feelings are acceptable. You might say, "It's okay to feel frustrated. Yelling and grabbing are not okay."

Parents and caregivers can set an example. If you feel tired, frustrated, proud, silly—talk about it. Show your child that no matter how you feel you can still be fair, considerate, and loving. Storybooks can be helpful with this as well. When reading books, ask your child what a character in the story might be feeling. Especially when problem-solving, encourage your child to think about the feelings of others.

Understanding a child's point of view is more important than fixing the problem. Be present, help label the feelings, be patient, and demonstrate acceptance (reserve judgment).

- That must have made you feel sad.
- I can understand why you felt that way.
- I can see you're really upset about losing the game.
- It sounds like you are very angry.

Look for dialogue in green for other examples of validating feelings.

Give Encouragement

Let kids know you are proud of their efforts by offering specific words of encouragement. Instead of saying, simply, "Good job!" notice and comment on what the child has done. "You shared your crayons with your friend," or "I noticed you took turns without arguing." Kids are much more likely to believe and react to specific encouragement.

Experts in child development point out that encouragement is different from praise. Praise—saying things like "Good job" or "Good girl"—conditions children to seek adults' approval rather than doing things for their own satisfaction. Praise focuses on the results of their efforts, assigns value to the results, and teaches kids they are only acceptable to you when they do well. Encouragement, on the other hand, focuses on their efforts and lets them know you love them and think they are important no matter how well they perform. For example, "You remembered to say please" encourages, whereas "Good job remembering your manners" praises.

Effective encouragement is also sincere. Here are some examples:

- You brushed your teeth without being asked.
- I noticed you waited for your turn patiently.
- I knew you could do it.
- You're really learning a lot.

Nonverbal gestures of encouragement also go a long way!

- a smile
- a pat on the shoulder or back
- a high five
- a hug

Look for dialogue in red for other examples of encouragement.

If the suggestions in this book feel unnatural or uncomfortable at first, try not to be intimidated! The mother in this story uses many techniques in a short period of time in order to provide plenty of examples of the language of positive parenting. As a first step, try using the technique that seems most natural and comfortable for you. Repeated use over time will make the language more comfortable and lead to better problem-solving and smoother playtime.

About the Author

Stacey R. Kaye, MMR, is the mother of two young children and a self-described "Parenting Lecture Groupie." As her first daughter grew into a feisty toddler, Stacey searched for a language she could use to discourage tantrums and meltdowns while at the same time encouraging her daughter to explore, grow confidence, and gain emotional intelligence. Dozens of parenting tomes, lectures, and courses provided great theory, but not the language. That's when Stacey began writing ParentSmart/KidHappy books.

To learn more positive parenting tips and discover other ParentSmart/KidHappy titles, visit **www.ParentSmartKidHappy.com**.

About the Illustrator

Award winning author/illustrator **Elizabeth O. Dulemba** was beamed to this planet with a pencil in her hand. Once she stopped chewing on it, she began to write and draw. She received her Bachelor of Fine Arts in Graphic Design from the University of Georgia and in 2001 began illustrating children's books. She now has several titles to her credit including the bilingual *Paco and the Giant Chile Plant* and *The Prince's Diary,* which Book Sense named the No. 1 Valentine's Day Pick of 2006. She enjoys sharing her passion for children's books at schools and events.

Elizabeth lives in Atlanta with her husband Stan, two big dogs, and a tiny cat who rules them all. Visit her Web site to learn more and download free coloring pages: **www.dulemba.com**.

Other Great Books from Free Spirit

Also in the ParentSmart/KidHappy™ Series

Ready for the Day!
A Tale of Teamwork and Toast, and Hardly Any Foot-Dragging
by Stacey R. Kaye, MMR, illustrated by Elizabeth O. Dulemba
Getting a preschooler out the door in the morning can be a frustrating battle of wills complete with crying and complaining—by parents and kids alike. *Ready for the Day!* offers a healthy, lasting solution. Share this kid-friendly storybook with your child and you'll both learn a new, positive way to get ready without stress. Replace the begging, bribing, and brawling with positive parenting. Learn how working with kids in a respectful, give-and-take relationship gets better results and helps kids grow from the inside out. For ages 3–6.
Hardcover; 32 pp.; color illust.; 8" x 8".

Ready for Bed!
A Tale of Cleaning Up, Tucking In, and Hardly Any Complaining
by Stacey R. Kaye, MMR, illustrated by Elizabeth O. Dulemba
"I don't *want* to go to bed!" If you're a parent of a preschool-age child, you've probably heard this before. And you probably know about the crying, fits, and complaining—by both of you—that can follow. *Ready for Bed!* offers a healthy, lasting solution. Share this kid-friendly storybook with your child and you'll both learn a new, positive way to get through bedtime. Replace the begging, bribing, and brawling with positive parenting. Learn how working with kids in a respectful, give-and-take relationship gets better results and helps kids grow from the inside out. For ages 3–6.
Hardcover; 32 pp.; color illust.; 8" x 8".

Free Spirit's Learning to Get Along® Series

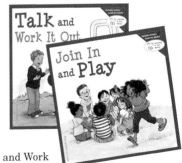

by Cheri J. Meiners, M.Ed.
Help children learn, understand, and practice basic social and emotional skills. Real-life situations, diversity, and concrete examples make these read-aloud books appropriate for childcare settings, schools, and the home. For ages 4–8.
Each book: Paperback; 40 pp.; color illust.; 9" x 9".

SERIES INCLUDES:

- Accept and Value Each Person
- Reach Out and Give
- Share and Take Turns
- Understand and Care
- Listen and Learn

- Be Careful and Stay Safe
- Try and Stick with It
- Know and Follow Rules
- When I Feel Afraid
- Join In and Play

- Talk and Work It Out
- Be Polite and Kind
- Be Honest and Tell the Truth
- Respect and Take Care of Things

From Free Spirit's Best Behavior™ Series

Hands Are Not for Hitting
by Martine Agassi, Ph.D., illustrated by Marieka Heinlen
Little ones learn that violence is never okay, hands can do many good things, and everyone is capable of positive, loving actions.
Paperback for ages 4–7. 40 pp.; color illust.; 9" x 9". Board book for ages baby–preschool. 24 pp.; color illust.; 7" x 7".

Words Are Not for Hurting
by Elizabeth Verdick, illustrated by Marieka Heinlen
Even very young children can learn that their words affect other people in powerful ways. This book guides them to choose words that are helpful instead of hurtful, and to say "I'm sorry" when hurtful words come out before kids can stop them.
Paperback for ages 4–7. 40 pp.; color illust.; 9" x 9". Board book for ages baby–preschool. 24 pp.; color illust.; 7" x 7".

free spirit
PUBLISHING®

217 Fifth Avenue North • Suite 200 • Minneapolis, MN 55401 • toll-free 800.735.7323
local 612.338.2068 • fax 612.337.5050 • help4kids@freespirit.com • **www.freespirit.com**

For pricing information, to place an order, or to request a free catalog, contact us.